Beginners Guide to Psychodynamic Therapy

Emerging Trends in Psychodynamic Therapy

By

Macallister Knox

Table of Contents

CHAPTER 1

Introduction

Psychotherapy, a diverse and dynamic field within the realm of mental health, serves as a vital means for individuals to address and alleviate psychological distress, enhance well-being, and foster personal growth. As an integral subset of psychotherapeutic modalities, psychodynamic therapy holds a unique place, drawing upon a rich tapestry of theoretical foundations and historical evolution.

1.1 Overview of Psychotherapy

Psychotherapy, broadly defined, is a collaborative and therapeutic interaction between a trained professional and an individual or group, aimed at resolving emotional, behavioral, and cognitive challenges. The overarching goal is to facilitate positive change, self-awareness, and improved mental health. The landscape of psychotherapy encompasses various theoretical orientations and approaches, each offering distinct perspectives on the human mind and its intricacies.

Within this expansive terrain, psychodynamic therapy stands out as a historically significant and enduring model. Rooted in the pioneering work of Sigmund Freud, psychodynamic therapy delves into the unconscious mind, emphasizing the role of early experiences, internal conflicts, and the dynamic interplay between conscious and unconscious processes. Unlike some more directive and short-term therapies, psychodynamic approaches often involve an exploration of long-standing patterns, encouraging clients to gain insight into the root causes of their thoughts, emotions, and behaviors.

The essence of psychodynamic therapy lies in the belief that understanding the unconscious factors influencing one's thoughts and actions can lead to profound personal transformation. Through a collaborative and reflective process, individuals engage in self-exploration, allowing the therapist to guide them in uncovering hidden motivations, unresolved conflicts, and the impact

of past experiences on their present
lives.

1.2 Historical Context of Psychodynamic Therapy

To appreciate the foundations of psychodynamic therapy, it is essential to delve into its historical context. The roots of this therapeutic approach trace back to the late 19th and early 20th centuries, a period marked by significant shifts in the understanding of the human mind and the emergence of psychoanalysis.

Sigmund Freud, often hailed as the father of psychoanalysis, laid the groundwork for psychodynamic theory. His exploration of the unconscious mind, the development of psychosexual stages, and the identification of defense mechanisms shaped the conceptual framework of psychodynamic therapy. Freud's revolutionary ideas challenged prevailing notions of consciousness and paved the way for a more nuanced understanding of human behavior.

As psychodynamic theory evolved, subsequent theorists, including Carl Jung, Alfred Adler, and Melanie Klein, contributed to its expansion and diversification. Each brought unique perspectives on the nature of the unconscious, the role of early experiences, and the dynamics of human relationships. Over time, psychodynamic therapy underwent refinements, incorporating insights from developmental psychology, attachment theory, and interpersonal dynamics.

The historical trajectory of psychodynamic therapy reflects not only theoretical evolution but also its adaptation to the changing landscape of mental health care. While contemporary psychotherapy encompasses a spectrum of modalities, psychodynamic therapy continues to exert a profound influence, demonstrating its enduring relevance and capacity to adapt to the complexities of the human psyche.

The overview of psychotherapy provides a broader context for understanding the multifaceted nature of therapeutic interventions, while the historical exploration of psychodynamic therapy unveils the rich tapestry of ideas and thinkers that have shaped its evolution. Together, these facets lay the groundwork for a comprehensive understanding of psychodynamic therapy, setting the stage for further exploration into its theoretical underpinnings, therapeutic techniques, and contemporary applications.

CHAPTER 2

Foundations of Psychodynamic Therapy

Psychodynamic therapy, deeply rooted in psychoanalytic traditions, rests upon a foundation of key theoretical concepts that illuminate the intricacies of the human psyche. This therapeutic approach seeks to unravel the unconscious forces shaping thoughts, emotions, and behaviors. Two fundamental pillars of psychodynamic theory are the concept of the unconscious mind and the theory of psychosexual development.

2.1 Key Theoretical Concepts

Unconscious Mind

At the heart of psychodynamic theory lies the profound and influential notion of the unconscious mind. Coined by Sigmund Freud, the unconscious represents a reservoir of thoughts, memories, desires, and emotions that exist beyond conscious awareness. It serves as a realm where repressed memories, unresolved conflicts, and instinctual drives reside, influencing behavior in ways individuals may not readily comprehend.

Psychodynamic therapists posit that much of human behavior is driven by unconscious processes. Exploration of the unconscious becomes a central focus of therapy, as clients work with therapists to bring hidden aspects of their psyche into conscious awareness. This process, known as psychoanalysis, involves techniques such as free association, dream analysis, and interpretation of symbols to uncover the latent content of thoughts and behaviors.

Understanding the unconscious mind is pivotal in psychodynamic therapy as it provides a gateway to self-discovery, enabling individuals to gain insight into the underlying factors contributing to their challenges and conflicts. By bringing these unconscious elements to light, clients can engage in a process of integration and transformation, fostering personal growth and emotional well-being.

Psychosexual Development

Another cornerstone of psychodynamic theory is the concept of psychosexual development, an intricate framework that elucidates the stages of human psychological maturation. Freud proposed a series of stages, each associated with a specific erogenous zone and developmental task. The stages include oral, anal, phallic, latent, and genital.

According to Freud, experiences and conflicts during these developmental stages profoundly shape an individual's personality and psychological functioning. The resolution of conflicts at each stage influences the formation of personality traits, coping mechanisms, and interpersonal relationships. For instance, unresolved conflicts during the phallic stage may lead to the development of defense mechanisms or contribute to issues related to sexuality and intimacy in adulthood.

In psychodynamic therapy, understanding an individual's psychosexual development provides a framework for comprehending present-day challenges and behaviors. Exploring how early experiences and conflicts manifest in current life allows therapists and clients to address underlying issues and work towards resolution and healing.

These key theoretical concepts, the unconscious mind, and psychosexual development, form the bedrock of psychodynamic therapy. Through the exploration of the unconscious and an understanding of developmental stages, psychodynamic therapists aim to unravel the complexities of the human psyche, offering a pathway to self-discovery, personal growth, and transformative change.

2.2 Freudian Principles

The Freudian principles form a pivotal aspect of psychodynamic therapy, delving into the structure of the human psyche and the dynamic interplay between its fundamental components. Developed by Sigmund Freud, these principles—comprising the id, ego, and superego—illuminate the intricate mechanisms that shape human behavior and personality. Additionally, the concept of defense mechanisms plays a crucial role in understanding how individuals navigate the often-conflicting demands of these internal entities.

2.2.1 Id, Ego, and Superego

2.2.1.1 *Id*

The id is the primal, instinctual aspect of the psyche, operating on the pleasure principle. It seeks immediate gratification of basic desires and urges, regardless of societal norms or consequences. The id is impulsive, irrational, and operates largely in the unconscious realm. It represents the innate drives for survival, pleasure, and avoidance of pain.

2.2.1.2 *Ego*

In contrast to the id, the ego operates on the reality principle. It serves as the executive mediator between the id's impulsive desires and the external world's demands. The ego employs rationality and problem-solving to find realistic ways of satisfying the id's demands while considering the constraints of the external environment. The ego strives for a balance between the id and external reality, making decisions that are both practical and socially acceptable.

2.2.1.3 *Superego*

The superego embodies the internalized moral and societal standards, serving as the conscience of the individual. It develops through the internalization of cultural and parental values during the process of socialization. The superego aims for perfection, striving for moral and ethical behavior. It often introduces feelings of guilt or shame when individuals deviate from societal or personal moral codes.

The interplay between the id, ego, and superego is dynamic and complex, influencing an individual's thoughts, emotions, and actions. Psychodynamic therapy involves exploring the conflicts and tensions between these elements, seeking a harmonious integration that fosters psychological well-being.

2.2.2 Defense Mechanisms

2.2.2.1 *Definition*

Defense mechanisms are psychological strategies employed by the ego to manage internal conflicts and protect the individual from distress. These mechanisms operate unconsciously and serve to reduce anxiety by distorting reality, regulating emotional responses, or redirecting unacceptable impulses.

2.2.2.2 *Examples of Defense Mechanisms*

- **Denial:** Refusing to acknowledge or accept a reality or truth.

- **Projection:** Attributing one's own unacceptable thoughts or feelings to another person.

- **Repression:** Unconsciously blocking out distressing thoughts or memories.

- **Regression:** Returning to earlier, more childlike patterns of behavior in stressful situations.

- **Rationalization:** Providing logical or reasonable explanations for behaviors that are actually driven by irrational motives.

Understanding defense mechanisms is integral to psychodynamic therapy as it sheds light on how individuals cope with internal conflicts and protect themselves from emotional distress. Therapists work collaboratively with clients to identify and explore these mechanisms, facilitating a deeper understanding of underlying issues and fostering healthier, more adaptive coping strategies.

Incorporating Freudian principles into psychodynamic therapy allows for a nuanced exploration of the internal dynamics that shape human behavior. By unraveling the complexities of the id, ego, and superego, as well as understanding the role of defense mechanisms, therapists and clients navigate the path towards self-awareness, personal growth, and psychological well-being.

CHAPTER 3

The Therapeutic Process

3.1 Assessment and Diagnosis

Before embarking on the therapeutic journey, a crucial and foundational phase involves the comprehensive assessment and diagnosis of the client's psychological well-being. This initial step is essential in tailoring the therapeutic approach to the individual's unique needs and challenges.

- **Comprehensive Assessment:** The assessment phase in psychodynamic therapy is thorough and multifaceted. It involves gathering information about the client's history, current life circumstances, interpersonal relationships, and presenting issues. Psychodynamic therapists pay particular attention to early childhood experiences and significant life events that may have shaped the client's personality and emotional landscape. The assessment may include interviews, standardized psychological tests, and self-report measures, offering a holistic understanding of the client's psychological functioning.

- **Exploration of Unconscious Processes:** Given the psychodynamic emphasis on the unconscious mind, the assessment process delves into uncovering hidden thoughts, emotions, and conflicts that may be influencing the client's behavior. Techniques such as free association, dream analysis, and projective assessments may be employed to reveal the deeper layers of the psyche. This exploration sets the stage for later phases of therapy, providing a foundation for self-awareness and insight.

- **Establishing a Therapeutic Alliance:** A crucial aspect of the assessment phase is the establishment of a strong therapeutic alliance. Psychodynamic therapists prioritize creating a safe and trusting relationship with the client. This alliance serves as the container for the therapeutic work to unfold, fostering an environment where the client feels comfortable exploring sensitive and often unconscious aspects of their experience.

3.2 Establishing the Therapeutic Alliance

- **Building Trust and Rapport:** Establishing a therapeutic alliance involves building trust and rapport between the client and therapist. Psychodynamic therapists recognize the significance of a secure and supportive relationship as a catalyst for change. Through empathetic listening, validation, and non-judgmental understanding, therapists create an atmosphere where clients feel heard and respected.

- **Mutual Collaboration:** The therapeutic process in psychodynamic therapy is a collaborative endeavor. Clients are encouraged to actively participate in their own self-exploration, and therapists guide them through the journey. The collaborative nature of the alliance empowers clients to take an active role in understanding and addressing their challenges, fostering a sense of agency and autonomy.

- **Transference and Countertransference:** A unique aspect of the therapeutic alliance in psychodynamic therapy is the exploration of transference and countertransference. Transference involves the client's unconscious transfer of emotions and attitudes from past relationships onto the therapist. Countertransference refers to the therapist's emotional reactions and responses to the client. By openly addressing and exploring these dynamics, psychodynamic therapists gain insights into deeper relational patterns and contribute to the therapeutic process.

Establishing a robust therapeutic alliance sets the stage for the unfolding exploration of unconscious processes and the collaborative work towards meaningful change. In psychodynamic therapy, the therapeutic alliance is not only a means to an end but an integral part of the therapeutic process, providing the foundation for self-discovery and transformation.

3.3 Techniques and Interventions

The therapeutic process in psychodynamic therapy is characterized by a diverse set of techniques and interventions designed to explore the unconscious mind, gain insight into deep-seated patterns, and facilitate transformative change. These techniques are rooted in the foundational principles of psychodynamic theory, emphasizing self-discovery and the resolution of unconscious conflicts.

3.3.1 Free Association

- **Definition:** Free association is
  a cornerstone technique in
  psychodynamic therapy,
  involving the spontaneous and
  uncensored verbal expression
  of thoughts, feelings, and
  images that come to mind.
  Clients are encouraged to speak
  freely, without self-censorship
  or concern for coherence. The
  goal is to access material from
  the unconscious, allowing
  hidden thoughts and emotions
  to surface.

- **Process:** During a therapy
  session, the client may start
  with a specific topic or a
  response to a therapist's
  prompt. As the client speaks,
  the therapist observes patterns,
  repetitions, and shifts in

content. Through free
association, clients may reveal
unconscious conflicts, desires,
and memories that contribute to
their current challenges. The
therapist, in turn, analyzes these
associations to gain insights
into the client's internal world.

- **Role in Therapy:** Free
association serves as a tool for
uncovering the latent content of
thoughts and emotions,
promoting self-awareness, and
facilitating the exploration of
unconscious material. It allows
the therapist and client to
collaboratively delve into the
depths of the psyche, bringing
hidden aspects into conscious
awareness for further
examination and understanding.

3.3.2 Dream Analysis

- **Significance:** Dream analysis is a technique that explores the symbolic content of dreams to gain insights into the unconscious mind. Freud believed that dreams were the "royal road to the unconscious" and that they contained disguised expressions of repressed desires, fears, and unresolved conflicts. Dream analysis is an avenue for understanding the symbolic language of the unconscious.

- **Process:** In psychodynamic therapy, clients are encouraged to share their dreams during sessions. The therapist and client collaboratively explore the symbols, emotions, and narratives within the dream.

Through this process, unconscious material that is typically inaccessible in waking life may come to the forefront. The therapist helps the client interpret the dream's symbolic content, connecting it to personal experiences and emotions.

- **Insight and Integration:** Dream analysis aims to uncover unconscious material, providing clients with insights into their inner conflicts and desires. By integrating the meanings of dreams into conscious awareness, individuals may gain a deeper understanding of their psychological landscape, contributing to the therapeutic journey.

3.3.3 Transference and Countertransference

- **Transference:** Transference involves the unconscious redirection of feelings and attitudes from past significant relationships onto the therapist. Clients may transfer emotions, such as love, anger, or dependency, onto the therapist, offering a window into unresolved issues from their past. Psychodynamic therapists actively explore transference dynamics as a means to understand and address deeper relational patterns.

- **Countertransference:** Countertransference refers to the therapist's emotional reactions and responses to the client, based on the therapist's own unresolved issues and past experiences. Psychodynamic therapists recognize countertransference as a valuable source of information about the therapeutic relationship and the client's impact on the therapist. Addressing and understanding countertransference enhances the therapeutic process.

- **Role in Therapy:** Transference and countertransference are not viewed as disturbances but as integral components of the therapeutic relationship. Exploring these dynamics allows the therapist and client to uncover unconscious material, relational patterns, and unresolved conflicts, fostering a deeper understanding of the client's internal world and contributing to the therapeutic process.

These techniques and interventions in psychodynamic therapy illustrate the commitment to exploring the depths of the unconscious, promoting self-awareness, and addressing unresolved conflicts. By engaging in free association, dream analysis, and navigating the complexities of transference and countertransference, psychodynamic therapists guide clients on a transformative journey towards self-discovery and emotional well-being.

CHAPTER 4

Applications and Effectiveness

4.1 Psychodynamic Therapy in Different Disorders

Psychodynamic therapy, with its focus on uncovering unconscious processes and exploring the intricacies of the human psyche, has demonstrated efficacy in addressing a range of psychological disorders. While it may not be the sole approach in all cases, its adaptability and depth make it a valuable therapeutic modality for various mental health conditions.

- **4.1.1 Anxiety Disorders:** Psychodynamic therapy is applied in the treatment of anxiety disorders, including generalized anxiety disorder, panic disorder, and social anxiety. By exploring the unconscious roots of anxiety, such as unresolved conflicts or repressed emotions, psychodynamic therapists help clients gain insight into the underlying causes of their anxiety and develop coping mechanisms.

- **4.1.2 Mood Disorders:** In the realm of mood disorders, such as depression and bipolar disorder, psychodynamic therapy addresses the interplay of unconscious factors that contribute to mood disturbances. The exploration of early life experiences, attachment patterns, and unresolved emotions can provide individuals with a deeper understanding of their emotional struggles, facilitating emotional expression and resilience.

- **4.1.3 Personality Disorders:** Psychodynamic therapy is frequently employed in the treatment of personality disorders, including borderline, narcissistic, and avoidant personality disorders. The focus on self-exploration and understanding deep-seated patterns of behavior is particularly relevant in addressing the core features of these disorders and fostering more adaptive ways of relating to oneself and others.

- **4.1.4 Eating Disorders:** When dealing with eating disorders like anorexia nervosa and bulimia nervosa, psychodynamic therapy delves into the complex relationship between unconscious conflicts, body image, and self-esteem. By exploring the roots of disordered eating behaviors, individuals can develop a more nuanced understanding of their struggles and work towards healthier relationships with food and their bodies.

- **4.1.5 Trauma and PTSD:** Psychodynamic therapy is applied in the treatment of trauma and post-traumatic stress disorder (PTSD). By addressing the impact of past traumatic experiences on the unconscious mind, therapists assist clients in processing and integrating traumatic memories. The therapeutic process aims to alleviate symptoms, enhance resilience, and promote post-traumatic growth.

- **4.1.6 Relationship Issues:** Psychodynamic therapy is well-suited for addressing relationship issues, including marital conflicts, difficulties in forming connections, and attachment issues. By exploring early attachment patterns and unconscious relational dynamics, individuals can gain insights into their relationship challenges and develop healthier ways of connecting with others.

- **4.1.7 Psychosomatic Disorders:** Psychodynamic therapy is applied in cases of psychosomatic disorders where physical symptoms are related to underlying psychological factors. By examining the connection between the mind and body, therapists assist clients in understanding how emotional distress may manifest as physical symptoms, contributing to a holistic approach to healing.

- **Effectiveness Across Disorders:** Research supports the effectiveness of psychodynamic therapy across various disorders. Meta-analyses and systematic reviews indicate that psychodynamic therapy can lead to significant improvements in symptoms, interpersonal functioning, and overall well-being. Its long-term focus on personal insight and change aligns with the idea that understanding the root causes of psychological distress can lead to lasting improvements.

psychodynamic therapy demonstrates versatility in its application across a spectrum of psychological disorders. By addressing unconscious processes and exploring the deeper layers of the human experience, psychodynamic therapists contribute to the understanding and treatment of diverse mental health challenges, fostering enduring positive change.

4.2 Criticisms and Controversies

While psychodynamic therapy has made significant contributions to the field of psychotherapy, it is not without its criticisms and controversies. As with any therapeutic approach, debates and concerns exist, reflecting varying perspectives within the mental health community. Here are some of the criticisms and controversies associated with psychodynamic therapy:

- **4.2.1 Lack of Empirical Support:** One of the primary criticisms centers around the perceived lack of empirical support for psychodynamic therapy. Critics argue that the approach's emphasis on subjective experiences and the unconscious makes it challenging to subject its techniques to rigorous scientific scrutiny. Some question the replicability and generalizability of findings, leading to debates about the empirical validation of psychodynamic concepts.

- **4.2.2 Length and Intensity of Treatment:** Psychodynamic therapy is often criticized for being lengthy and intensive compared to some short-term, structured therapies. The extended duration and frequency of sessions can be perceived as impractical for individuals seeking more immediate symptom relief. Critics argue that this may limit accessibility and affordability, especially for those with resource constraints.

- **4.2.3 Lack of Manualization:** Unlike some other therapeutic approaches that provide detailed treatment manuals, psychodynamic therapy is criticized for its relative lack of manualization. This lack of standardized protocols raises concerns about treatment consistency and fidelity. Critics argue that the variability in how therapists implement psychodynamic techniques may affect the reliability and comparability of research outcomes.

- **4.2.4 Limited Focus on Symptom Reduction:** Some critics contend that psychodynamic therapy's primary focus on exploring unconscious processes and gaining insight may not align with the contemporary emphasis on symptom reduction. Critics argue that more symptom-focused and evidence-based treatments might be better suited for addressing specific, targeted issues in a shorter time frame.

- **4.2.5 Subjectivity and Interpretation:** The subjective nature of interpretations in psychodynamic therapy has been a subject of criticism. Critics argue that the therapist's interpretations are highly subjective and open to multiple interpretations. This subjectivity can lead to challenges in establishing the reliability and validity of therapeutic insights, raising questions about the scientific rigor of psychodynamic practices.

- **4.2.6 Gender and Cultural Bias:** Historically, psychodynamic theory and therapy have been criticized for reflecting gender and cultural biases. Critics argue that early psychoanalytic theories, particularly those of Sigmund Freud, were rooted in a patriarchal and Eurocentric worldview. Efforts to address these biases have been made, but concerns persist about the cultural relevance and inclusivity of psychodynamic approaches.

- **4.2.7 Limited Attention to Behavioral Strategies:** Some critics argue that psychodynamic therapy may place less emphasis on the use of specific behavioral strategies and skills training compared to more behaviorally oriented therapies. This criticism is particularly relevant for individuals who benefit from structured interventions and practical skills development.

psychodynamic therapy, while influential and widely practiced, is not immune to criticism and controversy. The ongoing debates reflect the evolving nature of psychotherapy as a field, with diverse perspectives on the empirical validation, practicality, and cultural relevance of psychodynamic approaches. It is essential for practitioners and researchers to engage in ongoing dialogue to address these concerns and continue refining the application of psychodynamic principles in contemporary mental health care.

4.3 Research on the Effectiveness of Psychodynamic Therapy

Over the past several decades, there has been a growing body of research examining the effectiveness of psychodynamic therapy across a range of psychological disorders. While historical criticisms have focused on the perceived lack of empirical support, contemporary research has contributed to a more nuanced understanding of the therapeutic outcomes associated with psychodynamic approaches.

- **Empirical Support:** Contrary to earlier criticisms, a substantial body of research now supports the effectiveness of psychodynamic therapy. Numerous studies, including meta-analyses and systematic reviews, have reported positive outcomes in terms of symptom reduction, improved interpersonal functioning, and long-term psychological well-being.

- **Comparative Effectiveness:** Research has compared psychodynamic therapy with other therapeutic modalities, such as cognitive-behavioral therapy (CBT). Some studies suggest that psychodynamic therapy can be equally effective as other evidence-based approaches, especially in the treatment of complex and longstanding psychological issues. The choice between different therapies often depends on the nature of the presenting problems and the preferences of the client.

- **Long-Term Benefits:** Psychodynamic therapy is often associated with enduring benefits that extend beyond the completion of treatment. Research indicates that individuals who undergo psychodynamic therapy may experience sustained improvements in symptomatology and overall functioning. The focus on gaining insight and understanding underlying issues contributes to lasting changes in behavior and emotional well-being.

- **Neuroscientific Evidence:** Advances in neuroscientific research have provided additional insights into the mechanisms underlying psychodynamic therapy. Neuroimaging studies suggest that psychodynamic interventions can lead to changes in brain activity and connectivity, providing a neurobiological basis for the observed therapeutic effects. These findings contribute to a more comprehensive understanding of how

psychodynamic therapy
influences the brain.

- **Effectiveness Across Disorders:** Research has explored the application of psychodynamic therapy across various psychological disorders, including depression, anxiety, personality disorders, and trauma-related conditions. Positive outcomes have been reported in different clinical populations, supporting the versatility of psychodynamic approaches in addressing diverse mental health challenges.

- **Therapeutic Alliance:** The quality of the therapeutic alliance, a central component of psychodynamic therapy, has been identified as a key factor in treatment success. Research suggests that a strong therapeutic alliance correlates with positive treatment outcomes, emphasizing the importance of the therapeutic relationship in the effectiveness of psychodynamic therapy.

- **Integration with Other Modalities:** Some research has explored the integration of psychodynamic therapy with other therapeutic modalities, such as cognitive-behavioral and interpersonal therapies. Integrated approaches have shown promise in addressing a broader range of clinical issues and tailoring treatment to individual client needs.

While the research landscape supporting psychodynamic therapy has evolved, it is essential to note that the effectiveness of any therapeutic approach can be influenced by various factors, including the specific techniques used, the skills of the therapist, and the characteristics of the client. Ongoing research continues to refine our understanding of how and for whom psychodynamic therapy is most beneficial, contributing to the ongoing development of evidence-based practices in mental health care.

CHAPTER 5

Contemporary Approaches

5.1 Evolution of Psychodynamic Therapy

The field of psychodynamic therapy has undergone a significant evolution since its inception with Sigmund Freud's groundbreaking work. While maintaining its foundational principles, contemporary psychodynamic therapy reflects adaptations, integrations with other therapeutic modalities, and a broader perspective that aligns with current understandings of human psychology. Several key developments characterize the evolution of psychodynamic therapy:

- **5.1.1 Relational Psychodynamic Therapy:** Contemporary psychodynamic therapy places a strong emphasis on the therapeutic relationship and the interpersonal dynamics between the therapist and the client. Relational psychodynamic therapy acknowledges that the quality of the therapeutic alliance and the interaction between therapist and client play pivotal roles in the therapeutic process. This approach considers the therapeutic relationship as a microcosm for understanding and addressing relational patterns outside the therapy room.

- **5.1.2 Contemporary Psychoanalytic Schools:** The landscape of psychodynamic therapy now includes various contemporary psychoanalytic schools, each offering unique perspectives on theory and practice. Object relations theory, self-psychology, and interpersonal psychoanalysis are among the influential contemporary schools that have contributed to the diversification and refinement of psychodynamic approaches.

- **5.1.3 Short-Term and Time-Limited Psychodynamic Therapies:** In response to critiques about the length and intensity of traditional psychodynamic therapy, contemporary approaches include short-term and time-limited models. These adapted versions aim to provide more structured interventions while retaining the depth and insight associated with psychodynamic principles. Time-limited psychodynamic therapies often focus on specific goals within a predefined timeframe.

- **5.1.4 Integration with Cognitive-Behavioral Techniques:** Recognizing the importance of addressing specific symptoms and behavioral patterns, some contemporary psychodynamic therapists integrate cognitive-behavioral techniques into their practice. This integrative approach combines the depth and insight of psychodynamic therapy with the practical strategies and skills training inherent in cognitive-behavioral interventions.

- **5.1.5 Mindfulness and Psychodynamic Approaches:** Mindfulness practices have found their way into psychodynamic therapy, blending traditional psychodynamic principles with mindfulness-based techniques. This integration aims to enhance self-awareness, improve emotional regulation, and promote a non-judgmental exploration of thoughts and feelings. The incorporation of mindfulness aligns with broader trends in mental health care emphasizing holistic well-being.

- **5.1.6 Cultural Competence and Inclusivity:** Contemporary psychodynamic therapy recognizes the importance of cultural competence and inclusivity. Therapists are increasingly attuned to the impact of cultural factors on the therapeutic process and strive to create culturally sensitive and inclusive therapeutic environments. Efforts are made to address potential biases and ensure that psychodynamic therapy is accessible and relevant to individuals from diverse backgrounds.

- **5.1.7 Empirical Research and Evidence-Based Practice:** The evolution of psychodynamic therapy includes a growing emphasis on empirical research and evidence-based practice. Researchers and practitioners within the field actively contribute to studies assessing the efficacy and effectiveness of psychodynamic approaches across various disorders. This commitment to empirical validation enhances the credibility and integration of psychodynamic therapy within the broader mental health landscape.

The evolution of psychodynamic therapy reflects a dynamic response to changing clinical needs, advancements in psychological research, and an ongoing commitment to improving therapeutic outcomes. Contemporary approaches within the psychodynamic tradition demonstrate a flexibility that allows for integration with other therapeutic modalities, cultural responsiveness, and a focus on empirical validation, positioning psychodynamic therapy as a vibrant and evolving contributor to the field of psychotherapy.

5.2 Integration with Other Therapeutic Modalities

In response to the evolving landscape of mental health care and the recognition of diverse client needs, contemporary psychodynamic therapy has embraced an integrative approach, incorporating elements from other therapeutic modalities. This integration reflects a commitment to enhancing the flexibility and effectiveness of psychodynamic practice while acknowledging the value of various therapeutic perspectives. Several modalities have been particularly influential in shaping the integrated landscape of contemporary psychodynamic therapy:

- **5.2.1 Cognitive-Behavioral Therapy (CBT):** Integration with cognitive-behavioral therapy has been a notable development in contemporary psychodynamic practice. While traditionally distinct, the combination of psychodynamic and CBT techniques aims to address both the deeper, unconscious processes and the specific behaviors and thought patterns that contribute to psychological distress. This integrative approach is often referred to as psychodynamic-

CBT or psychodynamic cognitive therapy.

- **5.2.2 Mindfulness-Based Approaches:** Mindfulness practices, rooted in traditions such as Buddhism, have been integrated into psychodynamic therapy to enhance self-awareness, emotional regulation, and the exploration of present-moment experiences. The incorporation of mindfulness techniques aligns with psychodynamic principles by fostering a non-judgmental awareness of thoughts and feelings while promoting a deeper understanding of underlying psychological dynamics.

- **5.2.3 Dialectical Behavior Therapy (DBT):**

Psychodynamic therapy has integrated elements from Dialectical Behavior Therapy, particularly in the treatment of individuals with emotion dysregulation and borderline personality disorder. The combination of psychodynamic and DBT strategies addresses both the relational and emotional aspects of psychological difficulties, offering a more comprehensive approach to complex clinical presentations.

- **5.2.4 Humanistic and Existential Approaches:** Integrating humanistic and existential principles into psychodynamic therapy emphasizes the importance of individual growth, self-actualization, and existential exploration. This integration broadens the scope of psychodynamic work to include a focus on personal meaning, authenticity, and the pursuit of a fulfilling life.

- **5.2.5 Interpersonal Psychotherapy (IPT):** Drawing from interpersonal psychotherapy, contemporary psychodynamic therapists incorporate strategies that target specific interpersonal issues and relationship patterns. This integration enhances the relational focus of psychodynamic therapy and provides additional tools for addressing interpersonal challenges.

- **5.2.6 Attachment-Based Approaches:** Given the significance of attachment in psychodynamic theory, contemporary approaches integrate attachment-based perspectives to further understand relational dynamics. This integration emphasizes the impact of early attachment experiences on adult relationships and explores ways to enhance interpersonal functioning through a deeper understanding of attachment patterns.

- **5.2.7 Integrative Psychodynamic Models:** Some practitioners have developed integrative psychodynamic models that blend various therapeutic

approaches seamlessly. These
models aim to provide a
comprehensive and flexible
framework that incorporates
psychodynamic principles
alongside elements from other
evidence-based modalities.

- **5.2.8 Integrative Group Therapies:** In group therapy settings, psychodynamic approaches may be integrated with other therapeutic modalities to address diverse group dynamics. This integration allows for a more holistic understanding of individual and group processes, promoting interpersonal growth and mutual support.

The integration of psychodynamic
therapy with other modalities reflects
a recognition of the complexity of

human experience and the need for flexible, individualized approaches to treatment. This integrative stance positions contemporary psychodynamic therapy as a dynamic and responsive framework that draws on a diverse array of therapeutic tools to meet the unique needs of each client.

5.3 Emerging Trends in Psychodynamic Therapy

As the field of mental health continues to evolve, psychodynamic therapy adapts to emerging trends and incorporates innovative approaches. Several noteworthy trends are shaping the landscape of contemporary psychodynamic practice:

- **5.3.1 Integration of Technology:** The integration of

technology in psychodynamic therapy is on the rise. Therapists are utilizing video conferencing platforms for online sessions, expanding access to treatment and accommodating clients' diverse needs. Additionally, digital tools, such as mobile apps and virtual reality, are being explored to enhance therapeutic interventions and facilitate self-reflection.

- **5.3.2 Brief and Time-Limited Models:** While traditional psychodynamic therapy is often long-term, there is a growing interest in adapting the approach to brief and time-limited models. This trend aims to make psychodynamic principles more accessible and applicable to individuals seeking focused interventions for specific issues within a shorter time frame.

- **5.3.3 Neuroscientific Advances:** Advances in neuroscience contribute to a deeper understanding of the neurobiological mechanisms underlying psychodynamic processes. Neuroscientific research is informing the field, providing insights into how therapeutic interventions impact brain function and neural pathways, further validating the efficacy of psychodynamic therapy.

- **5.3.4 Cultural Sensitivity and Diversity:** The importance of cultural competence and inclusivity is increasingly emphasized in psychodynamic therapy. Therapists are recognizing the need to integrate cultural sensitivity into their practice, addressing diverse perspectives on identity, values, and relational dynamics. This trend aims to make psychodynamic therapy more relevant and accessible to individuals from various cultural backgrounds.

- **5.3.5 Interdisciplinary Collaboration:** Psychodynamic therapists are engaging in more interdisciplinary collaboration, working alongside professionals from fields such as neuroscience, sociology, and anthropology. This trend fosters a holistic understanding of human behavior and mental health, integrating insights from diverse disciplines into the psychodynamic framework.

- **5.3.6 Outcome Measurement and Research:** There is a growing emphasis on outcome measurement and research in psychodynamic therapy. Researchers are exploring ways to quantify therapeutic outcomes, assess treatment effectiveness, and contribute to the evidence base supporting psychodynamic approaches. This trend aligns with broader efforts to enhance the empirical foundation of psychotherapy.

- **5.3.7 Mind-Body Integration:** The integration of mind-body approaches is gaining attention within psychodynamic therapy.

Therapists are exploring the interconnectedness of psychological and physical well-being, incorporating techniques such as somatic experiencing and body-oriented interventions to address trauma and enhance overall therapeutic outcomes.

- **5.3.8 Accessibility and Telehealth:** This trend continues to shape the field, with therapists recognizing the benefits of telehealth in improving accessibility, reducing barriers to treatment, and accommodating the evolving preferences of clients.

- **5.3.9 Positive Psychology Integration:** The integration of positive psychology principles within psychodynamic therapy is an emerging trend. Therapists are incorporating strengths-based approaches, resilience-building strategies, and interventions that focus on enhancing well-being and fostering personal growth alongside traditional psychodynamic techniques.

- **5.3.10 Trauma-Informed Care:** A trauma-informed approach is increasingly emphasized within psychodynamic therapy. Therapists are incorporating trauma-informed principles to create safe and supportive therapeutic environments, recognizing the pervasive impact of trauma on mental health and addressing trauma-related issues within the psychodynamic framework.

These emerging trends reflect the dynamic nature of psychodynamic therapy as it evolves to meet the changing needs of individuals seeking mental health support. By embracing innovation, staying attuned to cultural considerations, and integrating insights from various disciplines, psychodynamic therapy remains a relevant and adaptable approach within the broader landscape of psychotherapy.

5.4 Research and Innovation in the Field

Research and innovation play crucial roles in advancing the field of psychodynamic therapy, contributing to its efficacy, understanding, and integration with contemporary mental health practices. Several notable areas of research and innovation are shaping the field:

- **5.4.1 Neuroscientific Exploration:** Ongoing neuroscientific research is shedding light on the neural mechanisms underlying psychodynamic processes. Advances in brain imaging techniques, such as functional magnetic resonance imaging (fMRI) and electroencephalography (EEG), provide insights into how psychodynamic interventions impact brain function and connectivity. This interdisciplinary approach enhances the scientific foundation of psychodynamic therapy.

- **5.4.2 Process and Outcome Research:** There is a continued focus on rigorous process and outcome research within the field of psychodynamic therapy. Studies aim to elucidate the specific therapeutic mechanisms, assess treatment effectiveness across diverse populations, and contribute to the growing evidence base supporting the efficacy of psychodynamic approaches. This research enhances the credibility of psychodynamic therapy within the broader mental health landscape.

- **5.4.3 Integration with Positive Psychology:** The integration of positive psychology principles into psychodynamic therapy is an area of innovation. Researchers are exploring how psychodynamic interventions can be enriched by incorporating positive psychology frameworks, strengths-based approaches, and interventions that promote well-being and resilience.

- **5.4.4 Comparative Effectiveness Studies:** Comparative effectiveness studies compare psychodynamic therapy with other therapeutic modalities, such as cognitive-behavioral therapy (CBT) or medication. These studies aim to provide clinicians and researchers with valuable information about the relative efficacy of psychodynamic approaches in comparison to other evidence-based treatments.

- **5.4.5 Technology-Assisted Interventions:** The use of technology in psychodynamic therapy is a growing area of innovation. Researchers are exploring the effectiveness of digital tools, mobile applications, virtual reality, and online platforms to enhance therapeutic interventions, improve accessibility, and support the delivery of psychodynamic therapy in diverse settings.

- **5.4.6 Trauma-Informed Innovations:** Innovations in trauma-informed care within psychodynamic therapy focus on developing specialized interventions for individuals with a history of trauma. Researchers are exploring trauma-specific approaches, such as EMDR (Eye Movement Desensitization and Reprocessing) within a psychodynamic framework, to address the unique needs of trauma survivors.

- **5.4.7 Adapting to Cultural Diversity:** Research is addressing the cultural relevance of psychodynamic therapy. This includes investigations into culturally adapted interventions, the impact of cultural factors on therapeutic processes, and strategies for enhancing cultural competence among psychodynamic therapists. Such research aims to make psychodynamic therapy more inclusive and responsive to diverse populations.

- **5.4.8 Innovations in Training Models:** Advances in training models for psychodynamic therapists are contributing to the professional development of practitioners. Innovations include the use of simulated or virtual reality-based training environments, online learning platforms, and mentorship models that enhance clinical skills and competencies.

- **5.4.9 Integration with Mind-Body Approaches:** The integration of mind-body approaches within psychodynamic therapy is explored in research initiatives. Studies investigate the impact of incorporating somatic experiencing, mindfulness practices, and other body-oriented interventions to enhance therapeutic outcomes, particularly in addressing trauma and stress-related disorders.

- **5.4.10 Hybrid and Integrative Models:** Researchers are exploring hybrid and integrative models that combine psychodynamic therapy with other evidence-based approaches. These innovative models aim to leverage the strengths of different therapeutic modalities, offering a tailored and flexible approach to meet the unique needs of clients.

As research and innovation continue to advance the field of psychodynamic therapy, practitioners benefit from a growing understanding of its underlying mechanisms, expanded treatment options, and increased adaptability to diverse client populations and emerging mental health challenges. This ongoing exploration contributes to the evolution and relevance of psychodynamic therapy within the broader landscape of psychotherapy.

5.5 The Continuing Relevance of Psychodynamic Therapy

Psychodynamic therapy, despite being one of the oldest forms of psychotherapy, maintains enduring relevance in the contemporary mental health landscape. Several factors contribute to its continued importance:

- **5.5.1 Depth of Understanding:** Psychodynamic therapy offers a unique depth of understanding by delving into the unconscious mind, exploring early life experiences, and uncovering hidden motivations. This comprehensive exploration contributes to a nuanced understanding of clients' thoughts, emotions, and behaviors, addressing the root causes of psychological distress.

- **5.5.2 Emphasis on the Therapeutic Relationship:** The therapeutic relationship is a cornerstone of psychodynamic therapy. The emphasis on building a strong and trusting alliance between therapist and client fosters a safe space for exploration and self-discovery. This relational focus contributes to the therapeutic process, providing a supportive foundation for addressing emotional challenges.

- **5.5.3 Holistic Approach:** Psychodynamic therapy takes a holistic approach to mental health, considering the interconnectedness of thoughts, emotions, behaviors, and relationships. By addressing the whole person, psychodynamic therapists aim to promote comprehensive healing and personal growth, recognizing the interplay between psychological, emotional, and social factors.

- **5.5.4 Adaptability to Diverse Issues:** Psychodynamic therapy's flexibility allows it to adapt to a wide range of psychological issues. Whether addressing long-standing patterns of behavior, current life stressors, or unresolved past traumas, psychodynamic principles can be applied to diverse clinical presentations, making it a versatile therapeutic approach.

- **5.5.5 Long-Term Impact:** The focus on gaining insight and understanding underlying patterns contributes to lasting changes in behavior and emotional well-being. Psychodynamic therapy's potential for enduring impact aligns with the growing recognition of the importance of sustained improvements in mental health over time.

- **5.5.6 Integration with Contemporary Approaches:** Psychodynamic therapy continues to evolve by integrating with contemporary approaches. The integration of cognitive-behavioral techniques, mindfulness practices, and positive psychology principles reflects its adaptability to incorporate elements that enhance its effectiveness and relevance in the current therapeutic landscape.

- **5.5.7 Cultural Sensitivity:** Efforts to enhance cultural competence within psychodynamic therapy contribute to its ongoing relevance. Therapists are increasingly attuned to the impact of cultural factors on the therapeutic process, making psychodynamic therapy more inclusive and responsive to the diverse needs of clients from various backgrounds.

- **5.5.8 Research Support:** A growing body of research

supports the effectiveness of psychodynamic therapy across various psychological disorders. Meta-analyses and systematic reviews demonstrate positive outcomes, contributing to the evidence base that underpins the continued use and recognition of psychodynamic therapy as a viable treatment option.

- **5.5.9 Focus on Meaning and Purpose:** Psychodynamic therapy addresses existential questions related to meaning, purpose, and the pursuit of a fulfilling life. This focus aligns with contemporary trends in mental health care that emphasize the importance of subjective well-being, personal growth, and the enhancement of overall life satisfaction.

- **5.5.10 Therapist's Personal Development:** The emphasis on the therapist's self-awareness and personal development is a distinctive feature of psychodynamic therapy. Therapists engaging in their own personal therapy contribute to their effectiveness and empathy, creating a model that values ongoing self-reflection and growth.

psychodynamic therapy's continuing relevance is rooted in its ability to provide a profound understanding of the human psyche, foster meaningful therapeutic relationships, and adapt to the evolving landscape of mental health care. As it integrates with contemporary approaches, maintains cultural sensitivity, and receives support from empirical research, psychodynamic therapy remains a valuable and enduring contributor to the field of psychotherapy.